20

STUDY GUIDE

International Relations: Who Was to Blame for the Cold War?

CIE

app
available

Published by Clever Lili Limited.

contact@cleverlili.com

First published 2020

ISBN 978-1-913887-19-3

Cover by: Unknown author on Wikimedia Commons

Icons by: flaticon and freepik

Contributors: Lynn Harkin, Nicola Nicholls, Jonathan Boyd, Megan Quirk, Jen Mellors

Edited by Paul Connolly and Rebecca Parsley

Design by Evgeni Veskov and Will Fox

DISCOVER MORE OF OUR IGCSE HISTORY STUDY GUIDES

GCSEHistory.com and Clever Lili

CIE
STUDY GUIDE
International Relations:
Were the Peace Treaties of 1919–23 Fair?
GCSEHistory.com
17

CIE
STUDY GUIDE
International Relations:
To What Extent Was the League of Nations a Success?
GCSEHistory.com
18

CIE
STUDY GUIDE
International Relations:
Why Had International Peace Collapsed by 1939?
GCSEHistory.com
19

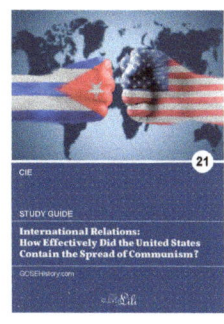

CIE
STUDY GUIDE
International Relations:
How Effectively Did the United States Contain the Spread of Communism?
GCSEHistory.com
21

CIE
STUDY GUIDE
International Relations:
How Secure Was the USSR's Control Over Eastern Europe, 1948 - 1989?
GCSEHistory.com
22

CIE
STUDY GUIDE
International Relations:
Why Did Events in the Gulf Matter c1970 - 2000?
GCSEHistory.com
23

CIE
STUDY GUIDE
The United States, 1919 - 1941
GCSEHistory.com
32

CIE
STUDY GUIDE
The First World War, 1914 - 1918
GCSEHistory.com
31

CIE
STUDY GUIDE
Russia, 1905 - 1941
GCSEHistory.com
33

CIE
STUDY GUIDE
Germany, 1918 - 1945
GCSEHistory.com
34

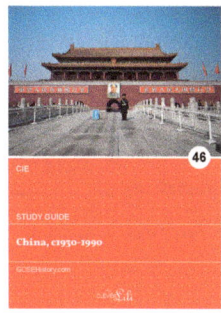

CIE
STUDY GUIDE
China, c1930-1990
GCSEHistory.com
46

THE GUIDES ARE EVEN BETTER WITH OUR GCSE/IGCSE HISTORY WEBSITE APP AND MOBILE APP

GCSE History is a text and voice web and mobile app that allows you to easily revise for your GCSE/IGCSE exams wherever you are - it's like having your own personal GCSE history tutor. Whether you're at home or on the bus, GCSE History provides you with thousands of convenient bite-sized facts to help you pass your exams with flying colours. We cover all topics - with more than 120,000 questions - across the Edexcel, AQA and CIE exam boards.

Contents

In this study guide, you will see a series of icons, highlighted words and page references. The key below will help you quickly establish what these mean and where to go for more information.

Icons

WHAT questions cover the key events and themes.

WHO questions cover the key people involved.

WHEN questions cover the timings of key events.

WHERE questions cover the locations of key moments.

WHY questions cover the reasons behind key events.

HOW questions take a closer look at the way in which events, situations and trends occur.

IMPORTANCE questions take a closer look at the significance of events, situations, and recurrent trends and themes.

DECISIONS questions take a closer look at choices made at events and situations during this era.

Highlighted words

Abdicate - occasionally, you will see certain words highlighted within an answer. This means that, if you need it, you'll find an explanation of the word or phrase in the glossary which starts on **page 39**.

Page references

Tudor *(p.7)* - occasionally, a certain subject within an answer is covered in more depth on a different page. If you'd like to learn more about it, you can go directly to the page indicated.

The focus question of the fourth unit in the CiE Option B Core Content is 'Who was to blame for the Cold War?' This unit investigates the breakdown of the relationship between the USA and USSR after the Second World War, and the impact of events between 1945 and 1949 on the development of the Cold War.

Purpose
This unit focuses on international relations and the way in which different nation states interacted, and the change, continuity and significance of their relationships over time. You will study their priorities, agreements, disagreements and the key events that affected them.

Enquiries
This unit gives you the information you need to understand the following:

- Why the US-Soviet alliance had begun to break down in 1945.
- How the USSR gained control of eastern Europe by 1948.
- How the US reacted to Soviet expansionism.
- The consequences of the Berlin Blockade.
- Whether the US or USSR was more to blame for the outbreak of the Cold War.

Topics
Topics covered in this course include:

- The Grand Alliance of the Second World War.
- The Tehran, Yalta and Potsdam conferences.
- Churchill's 'Iron Curtain' speech.
- The Long Telegram.
- The Truman Doctrine.
- The Marshall Plan.
- Soviet expansion into eastern Europe.
- The creation of Cominform and Comecon.
- NATO and the Warsaw Pact.
- The Berlin Blockade and Airlift.
- The arms race.
- The question of blame in the start of the Cold War.

Key Individuals
Key individuals studied in this course include:

- Franklin S Roosevelt.
- Harry S Truman.
- Winston Churchill.
- Joseph Stalin.
- George Kennan.
- George Marshall.

Assessment
This unit usually appears as one of four possible questions in Option B Core Content International Relations Since 1919 on the Paper 1 exam, of which you must complete two. Therefore, you will answer one question on the causes of the Cold War, if this appears as an option on your exam paper. The question is comprised of 3 sections; a), b), and c). However, check with your teacher to find out whether this unit will appear on the Paper 2 source paper in your exam.

- On the Paper 1 exam, you may choose to complete a three-part question on this topic, which will be divided into sections a), b) and c).
- Question a is worth 4 marks. This question will require you to describe key features of the time period. You will be asked to recall 2 relevant points and support them with details or provide at least four relevant points without supporting detail.

Question b is worth 6 marks. This question will require you to explain a key event or development. You will need to identify two reasons, support those reasons with relevant factual detail and then explain how the reasons made the event occur.

Question c is worth 10 marks. This question will require you to construct an argument to support and challenge an interpretation stated in the question. You will need to have a minimum of three explanations (two on one side of the argument and one on the other side) in total, fully evaluate the argument and come to a justified conclusion. You will have the opportunity to show your ability to explain and analyse historical events using 2nd order concepts such as causation, consequence, change, continuity, similarity and difference.

If this topic appears on Paper 2, you will answer six questions on a range of source material about this topic. Check with your teacher to find out your Paper 2 topic.

Revision! A dreaded word. Everyone knows it's coming, everyone knows how much it helps with your exam performance, and everyone struggles to get started! We know you want to do the best you can in your IGCSEs, but schools aren't always clear on the best way to revise. This can leave students wondering:

- ✔ How should I plan my revision time?
- ✔ How can I beat procrastination?
- ✔ What methods should I use? Flash cards? Re-reading my notes? Highlighting?

Luckily, you no longer need to guess at the answers. Education researchers have looked at all the available revision studies, and the jury is in. They've come up with some key pointers on the best ways to revise, as well as some thoughts on popular revision methods that aren't so helpful. The next few pages will help you understand what we know about the best revision methods.

How can I beat procrastination?

This is an age-old question, and it applies to adults as well! Have a look at our top three tips below.

◎ Reward yourself

When we think a task we have to do is going to be boring, hard or uncomfortable, we often put if off and do something more 'fun' instead. But we often don't really enjoy the 'fun' activity because we feel guilty about avoiding what we should be doing. Instead, get your work done and promise yourself a reward after you complete it. Whatever treat you choose will seem all the sweeter, and you'll feel proud for doing something you found difficult. Just do it!

◎ Just do it!

We tend to procrastinate when we think the task we have to do is going to be difficult or dull. The funny thing is, the most uncomfortable part is usually making ourselves sit down and start it in the first place. Once you begin, it's usually not nearly as bad as you anticipated.

◎ Pomodoro technique

The pomodoro technique helps you trick your brain by telling it you only have to focus for a short time. Set a timer for 20 minutes and focus that whole period on your revision. Turn off your phone, clear your desk, and work. At the end of the 20 minutes, you get to take a break for five. Then, do another 20 minutes. You'll usually find your rhythm and it becomes easier to carry on because it's only for a short, defined chunk of time.

Spaced practice

We tend to arrange our revision into big blocks. For example, you might tell yourself: "This week I'll do all my revision for the Cold War, then next week I'll do the Medicine Through Time unit."

This is called **massed practice**, because all revision for a single topic is done as one big mass.

But there's a better way! Try **spaced practice** instead. Instead of putting all revision sessions for one topic into a single block, space them out. See the example below for how it works.

This means planning ahead, rather than leaving revision to the last minute - but the evidence strongly suggests it's worth it. You'll remember much more from your revision if you use **spaced practice** rather than organising it into big blocks. Whichever method you choose, though, remember to reward yourself with breaks.

Spaced practice (more effective):

week 1	week 2	week 3	week 4
Topic 1	Topic 1	Topic 1	Topic 1
Topic 2	Topic 2	Topic 2	Topic 2
Topic 3	Topic 3	Topic 3	Topic 3
Topic 4	Topic 4	Topic 4	Topic 4

Massed practice (less effective)

week 1	week 2	week 3	week 4
Topic 1	Topic 2	Topic 3	Topic 4

What methods should I use to revise?

Self-testing/flash cards

Self explanation/mind-mapping

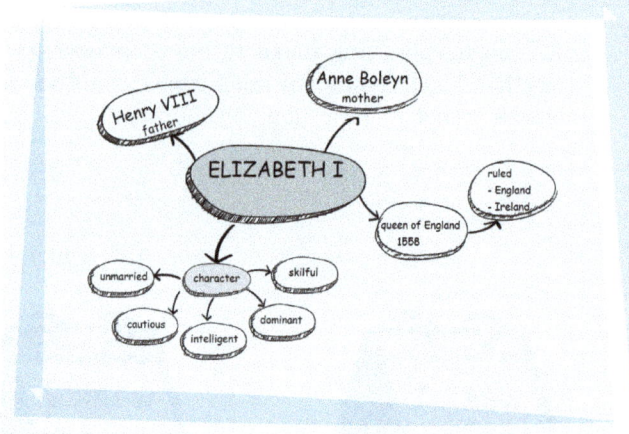

The research shows a clear winner for revision methods - **self-testing**. A good way to do this is with ==flash cards.== Flash cards are really useful for helping you recall short – but important – pieces of information, like names and dates.

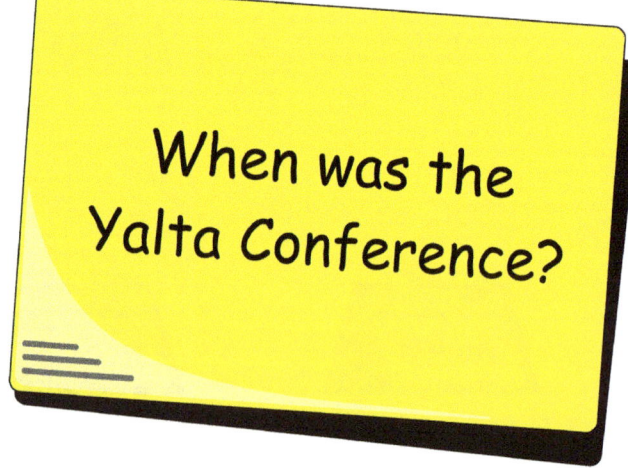

Side A - question

Side B - answer

Write questions on one side of the cards, and the answers on the back. This makes answering the questions and then testing yourself easy. Put all the cards you get right in a pile to one side, and only repeat the test with the ones you got wrong - this will force you to work on your weaker areas.

pile with right answers

pile with wrong answers

As this book has a quiz question structure itself, you can use it for this technique.

Another good revision method is **self-explanation**. This is where you explain how and why one piece of information from your course linked with another piece.

This can be done with ==mind-maps,== where you draw the links and then write explanations for how they connect. For example, President Truman is connected with anti-communism because of the Truman Doctrine.

Quizzes, amazing exam preparation tools and more at GCSEHistory.com

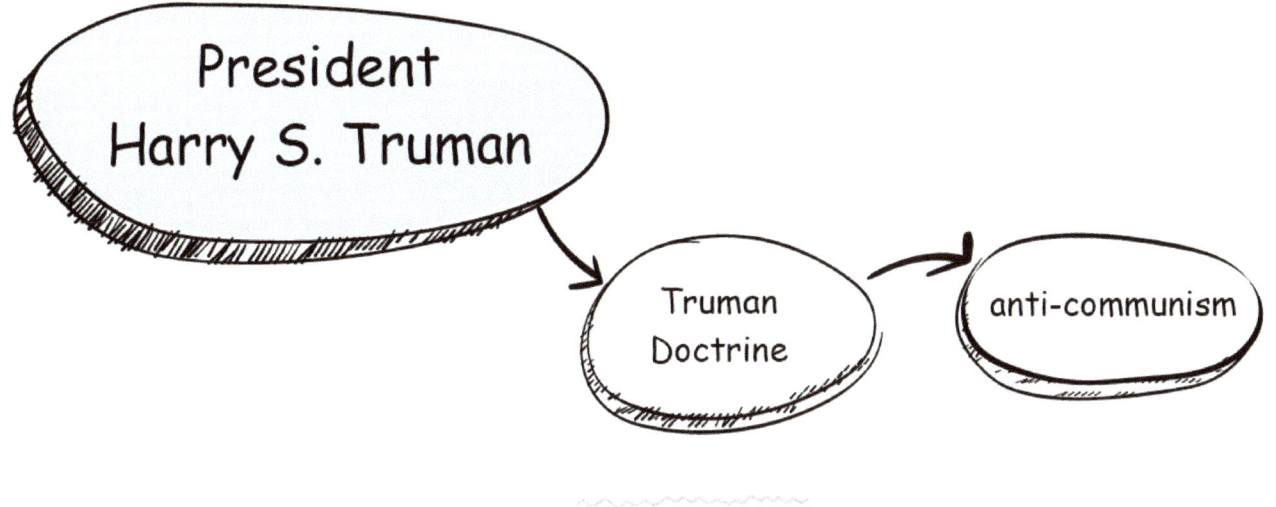

Review

Start by highlighting or re-reading to create your flashcards for self-testing.

Self-Test

Test yourself with flash cards. Make mind maps to explain the concepts.

Apply

Apply your knowledge on practice exam questions.

Which revision techniques should I be cautious about?

Highlighting and **re-reading** are not necessarily bad strategies - but the research does say they're less effective than flash cards and mind-maps.

Highlighting

Re-reading

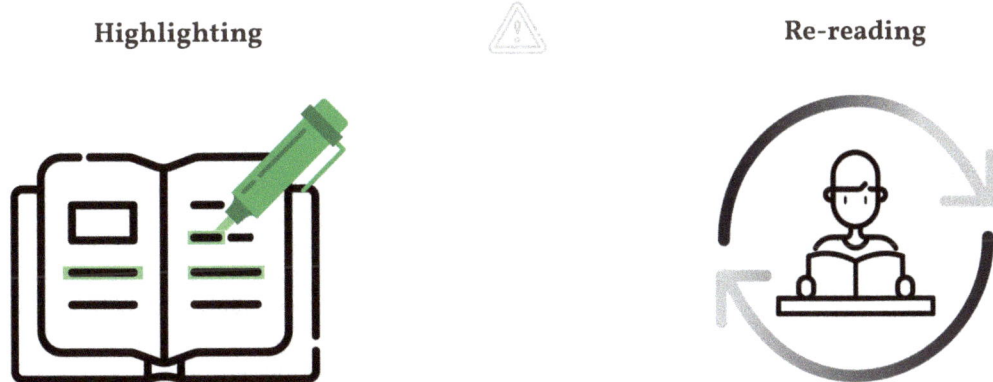

If you do use these methods, make sure they are **the first step to creating flash cards**. Really engage with the material as you go, rather than switching to autopilot.

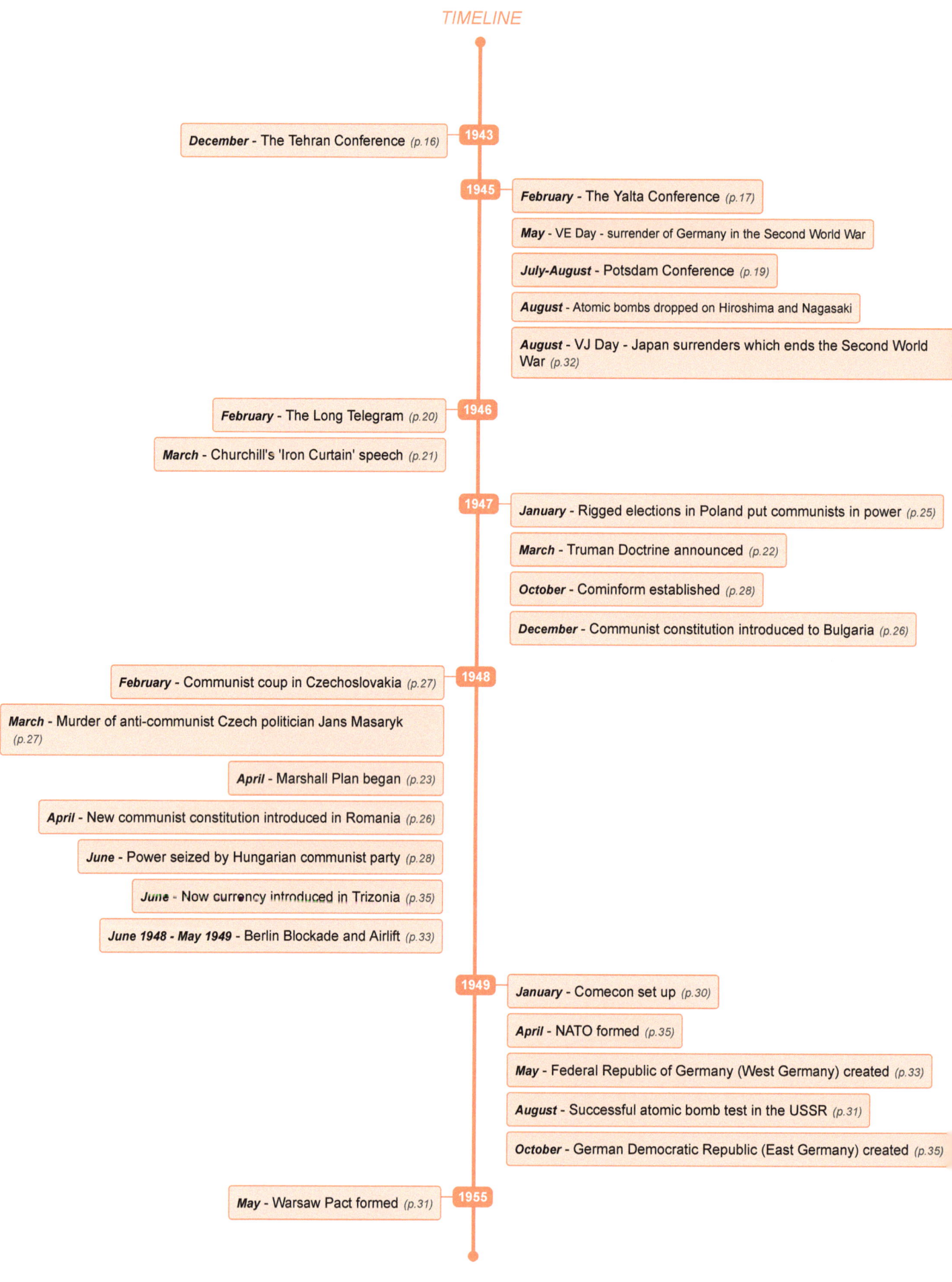

TIMELINE

December - The Tehran Conference *(p.16)*

1943

1945

February - The Yalta Conference *(p.17)*

May - VE Day - surrender of Germany in the Second World War

July-August - Potsdam Conference *(p.19)*

August - Atomic bombs dropped on Hiroshima and Nagasaki

August - VJ Day - Japan surrenders which ends the Second World War *(p.32)*

February - The Long Telegram *(p.20)*

1946

March - Churchill's 'Iron Curtain' speech *(p.21)*

1947

January - Rigged elections in Poland put communists in power *(p.25)*

March - Truman Doctrine announced *(p.22)*

October - Cominform established *(p.28)*

December - Communist constitution introduced to Bulgaria *(p.26)*

February - Communist coup in Czechoslovakia *(p.27)*

1948

March - Murder of anti-communist Czech politician Jans Masaryk *(p.27)*

April - Marshall Plan began *(p.23)*

April - New communist constitution introduced in Romania *(p.26)*

June - Power seized by Hungarian communist party *(p.28)*

June - Now currency introduced in Trizonia *(p.35)*

June 1948 - May 1949 - Berlin Blockade and Airlift *(p.33)*

1949

January - Comecon set up *(p.30)*

April - NATO formed *(p.35)*

May - Federal Republic of Germany (West Germany) created *(p.33)*

August - Successful atomic bomb test in the USSR *(p.31)*

October - German Democratic Republic (East Germany) created *(p.35)*

May - Warsaw Pact formed *(p.31)*

1955

TIMELINE

THE COLD WAR

'Although the shooting war is over, we are in the midst of a cold war which is getting warmer.'
Bernard Baruch, 1947

What was the Cold War?

The Cold War was a state of hostility that existed between the USSR and the USA in the second half of the 20th century.

What is the definition of a cold war?

A cold war is a conflict in which there is no direct fighting between the two sides. It is fought through economic and political actions.

When was the Cold War?

The Cold War lasted from 1945 to 1991.

Who was involved in the Cold War?

The Cold War was between the USA and its allies, and the Soviet Union, its satellite states and its allies.

What were the long-term causes of the Cold War?

There are 7 main reasons the Cold War happened:

- ☑ In October 1917, the Bolsheviks seized power in Russia. By 1921 they had created the first communist state. They were anti-capitalism and wanted to spread the communist revolution across the world.
- ☑ America and Britain did not trust the USSR as Russia had withdrawn from the First World War in 1917, despite being a member of the Triple Entente with Britain and France.
- ☑ The USSR did not trust the USA, France and Britain because they sent troops to fight against the Bolsheviks in the Russian Civil War.
- ☑ In the 1920s, the USA suffered from the First Red Scare and was hostile towards the USSR.
- ☑ The USSR was angry it was not recognised as a country by the USA until 1933.
- ☑ The relationship between the USSR and the West deteriorated before the Second World War. The Soviet Union was angry at not being invited to the Munich Conference in 1938.
- ☑ When the USSR signed the Nazi-Soviet Pact in 1939, Britain and France were horrified.

How was the Cold War fought?

The Cold War was fought in 7 key ways:

- ☑ Propaganda.
- ☑ Spying or espionage, such as using spy planes to take photographs.
- ☑ An arms race to have the most developed weapons, particularly nuclear missiles.
- ☑ A space race competing for success in space, such as being the first nation to put a man on the moon.
- ☑ Financial aid or loans to other countries to gain their support.
- ☑ Proxy wars, where the USA and the USSR became involved in conflicts in other countries. An example is the Korean War of 1950-53.
- ☑ Threats made by either side.

What created tension between the Soviet Union and the USA at the beginning of the Cold War?

The ideological differences between the superpowers created tension between them. The Soviet Union supported communism, whereas the USA and Britain were capitalist countries.

What were the different ideologies in the Cold War?

The Cold War was a result of ideological differences between the two sides:

☑ The USSR was communist. Communism is a system where there is no private ownership of land, property or business. The aim is to achieve economic equality for the benefit of the people through central control of the state economy.

☑ The USA was capitalist. Capitalism is a system where individuals are free to own land, property and businesses to create wealth and accept there will be economic inequality as a result.

Why were the USA and the USSR considered superpowers during the Cold War?

The USSR and the USA were considered to be superpowers because they possessed 3 key things:

☑ Massive military might, including nuclear weapons.

☑ Economic might.

☑ The ability to dominate other countries.

Why was Stalin distrustful of Truman at the beginning at the Cold War?

Joseph Stalin was distrustful of Harry S Truman for 3 key reasons:

☑ Truman was anti-communist.

☑ He tried to control the Potsdam meeting.

☑ He successfully tested the atomic bomb without consulting Stalin and used it in the Hiroshima and Nagasaki bombings in the days after Potsdam.

Why did Britain ally closely with the USA at the beginning at the Cold War?

Britain was concerned about communism spreading. The nation's economy was severely impacted after the Second World War so it couldn't act against the Soviet Union alone.

DID YOU KNOW?

The first known mention of the term 'Cold War' was by the English author, George Orwell.

He mentioned it in an essay entitled 'You and the Atomic Bomb', written in 1945.

THE GRAND ALLIANCE IN THE SECOND WORLD WAR

'If Hitler invaded Hell I would make at least a favourable reference to the Devil in the House of Commons.'
Winston Churchill 1950

What was the Grand Alliance?

The Grand Alliance was a military and political coalition against the Axis powers of Nazi Germany, Italy, and Japan during the Second World War.

When was the Grand Alliance formed?

The Grand Alliance began after the USA entered the Second World War. The alliance was formally signed by the USA, the Soviet Union and Great Britain on New Year's Day, 1942, and lasted until 1945.

Who was part of the Grand Alliance?

The Grand Alliance consisted of the three major Allies of the Second World War - the Soviet Union, the United States, and Great Britain.

Why was the Grand Alliance formed?

The sole purpose of the Grand Alliance was to defeat the Axis powers - Nazi Germany, fascist Italy and Imperial Japan.

Why was there tension in the Grand Alliance?

Although they were fighting the Nazi threat together, there were 3 main reasons for tension between the countries of the Grand Alliance during the Second World War:

- ☑ Both sides kept secrets. Stalin refused to share battle plans with Britain and France; when German troops surrendered in Italy, Britain and the US did not include the USSR in the discussions.
- ☑ Stalin believed the USA had deliberately delayed opening a second front in France until 1944 so the USSR would be weakened fighting Nazi Germany on its own.
- ☑ The two sides had opposing ideologies and did not trust each other.

How did the Grand Alliance cooperate during the Second World War?

The public was presented with a positive image of the Grand Alliance, and the three countries did help each other in 3 key ways:

- ☑ British merchant ships helped take supplies to the USSR.
- ☑ America included the USSR in its Lend-Lease programme, which meant it lent and sold military equipment to help defeat Germany.
- ☑ The USSR lost 26 million people fighting the Nazis after 1941, but this meant Germany's army was tied down and allowed Britain and America to plan and launch D-Day.

DID YOU KNOW?

At first, Stalin and Churchill apparently got on well together on a personal level.

According to a senior diplomat at the Moscow Conference in 1942, he found Churchill and Stalin 'surrounded by numerous bottles... as merry as a marriage bell'.

THE TEHRAN CONFERENCE, NOVEMBER-DECEMBER 1943

'The supreme responsibility resting upon us... to banish the scourge and terror of war for many generations.'
Joint Declaration by Roosevelt, Churchill and Stalin, December 1943

What was the Tehran Conference?

The Tehran Conference was the first of three strategic meetings between the USA, Britain and the Soviet Union to discuss Nazi Germany and how to end the war.

Who attended the Tehran Conference?

The three Allied leaders who attended the Tehran Conference were:

- ☑ President Franklin D Roosevelt of the United States.
- ☑ General Secretary Joseph Stalin of the USSR.
- ☑ Prime Minister Winston Churchill of the United Kingdom.

Where was the Tehran Conference held?

It was held at the Soviet Union's embassy in Tehran, Iran.

When was the Tehran Conference held?

The Tehran Conference was held from November to December, 1943.

Why was the Tehran Conference important?

The Tehran Conference was important for 3 main reasons:

- ☑ It led to a better relationship between the USA, Britain and the USSR.
- ☑ They were working together to defeat Nazi Germany, fascist Italy and Imperial Japan.
- ☑ They also discussed plans for the UN and ending the war.

What decisions were taken at the Tehran Conference?

There were 5 important decisions made at the Tehran Conference:

- ☑ It was decided the USA and Britain would open a second front by invading Europe through Nazi-occupied France.
- ☑ The USSR would invade Nazi Germany from the east.
- ☑ The USSR would invade Japan once Nazi Germany was defeated.
- ☑ The Polish border would be moved to the west, so Poland would gain territory from Germany and lose it to the USSR from the east.
- ☑ An international organisation would be created to settle international disagreements once the war was over. This would eventually become the United Nations.

What signs of tension were there at the Tehran Conference?

There were 2 key signs of tension at the Tehran Conference:

- ☑ Churchill wanted the second front to be opened up in the Balkans, not in France.
- ☑ Roosevelt viewed Britain's colonialism as a greater threat than communism.

DID YOU KNOW?

Although they had spoken with each other individually, the Tehran Conference was the first time that Churchill, Roosevelt and Stalin met at the same time.

THE YALTA CONFERENCE, FEBRUARY 1945

'I can deal with Stalin. He is honest, but smart as hell.'
President Harry Truman, 1945

What was the Yalta Conference?

The Yalta Conference was the second of three strategic meetings between the USA, Britain and the Soviet Union to discuss winning the war and post-war Europe.

Where was the Yalta Conference held?

The Yalta Conference took place in Yalta in the USSR.

When was the Yalta Conference held?

The Yalta Conference was held in February 1945.

Who attended the Yalta Conference?

The three Allied leaders present at the Yalta Conference were:

- ✅ President Roosevelt of the USA.
- ✅ General Secretary Stalin of the USSR.
- ✅ Prime Minister Churchill of Great Britain.

What decisions were taken at the Yalta Conference?

There were 11 important decisions made at the Yalta Conference.

- ✅ The superpowers agreed on the Declaration of Liberated Europe which guaranteed all countries freed from Nazi control the right to hold democratic and free elections.
- ✅ Nazi Germany and Berlin would be divided into four zones controlled by the USA, Britain, France and the Soviet Union.
- ✅ Germany would be reduced in size.
- ✅ Germany would be demilitarised.
- ✅ Germany would be ordered to pay reparations.
- ✅ Nazi war criminals would be tried after the war was over and the Nazi Party banned.
- ✅ Poland would fall under the Soviet sphere of influence.
- ✅ Poland would be run under a democratically elected government.
- ✅ Eastern Europe would have free elections.
- ✅ The USSR would declare war on Japan 3 months after Nazi Germany was defeated.
- ✅ The United Nations was created.

What disagreements were there at the Yalta Conference?

There were 3 main disagreements at the Yalta Conference:

- ✅ The USSR wanted Germany to pay high reparations; Britain and the USA disagreed.
- ✅ Britain and the USA wanted Germany to recover, whereas the USSR wanted to keep Germany weak.
- ✅ Stalin wanted the Polish-German border to be much further to the west and desired a 'friendly' Polish government. Britain and the USA were worried this would mean Poland would be controlled by the USSR.

DID YOU KNOW?

At the Yalta Conference, Stalin apologised for the Nazi-Soviet Pact and the partition of Poland.

Quizzes, amazing exam preparation tools and more at GCSEHistory.com

THE POTSDAM CONFERENCE, JULY 1945

'Unless Russia is faced with an iron fist and strong language, another war is in the making.'
President Harry Truman, 1946

What was the Potsdam Conference?

The Potsdam Conference was the third and final meeting between the USA, Britain and the Soviet Union to discuss Nazi Germany and the future of Europe.

Where was the Potsdam Conference held?

The Potsdam Conference was held in Potsdam, Germany.

When was the Potsdam Conference held?

The Potsdam Conference took place between July and August 1945.

Who attended the Potsdam Conference?

The three Allied leaders who met at Potsdam were:

- ☑ President Harry Truman of the United States.
- ☑ Prime Minister Clement Attlee of Great Britain.
- ☑ Premier Joseph Stalin of the Soviet Union.

Why did the leaders at the Potsdam Conference change?

Leadership of two Allied nations had changed since the Yalta Conference *(p.17)*. Roosevelt died in April 1945 and Churchill lost the British general election in July.

What disagreements were there at the Potsdam Conference?

There were 4 key areas of disagreement:

- ☑ The USA and Britain were unhappy Stalin had removed the non-communists from the Polish Provisional Government of National Unity.
- ☑ The USA and Britain were unhappy Stalin had not allowed free elections in eastern Europe. Stalin was angry as he thought the West was interfering.
- ☑ Truman deliberately delayed the Potsdam meeting so America could test the atomic bomb. When Truman informed Stalin about the USA's successful test, Stalin was very angry not to have been told beforehand.
- ☑ Truman was very anti-communist and wanted to get 'tough' with Stalin.

What decisions were taken at the Potsdam Conference?

There were 8 important decisions made at the Potsdam Conference:

- ☑ The Nazi Party was banned.
- ☑ War criminals were to be prosecuted.
- ☑ Germany was to be reduced in size.
- ☑ Germany would be divided into four occupied zones controlled by the USA, Britain, France and the Soviet Union.
- ☑ Berlin would also be divided into four occupied zones controlled by the USA, Britain, France and the Soviet Union.
- ☑ All economic decisions about Germany must be agreed to by all four powers in the Allied Control Council.
- ☑ A Council of Foreign Ministers was set up to organise the rebuilding of Europe.
- ☑ It was decided the Soviet Union would receive 25% of the industrial output from the other three occupied zones.

THE LONG TELEGRAM, 1946

'The main element of any United States policy toward the Soviet Union must be that of a long-term, patient but firm and vigilant containment...'
George Kennan, 1947

What was the 'Long Telegram'?

The Long Telegram was a secret report sent by the US Ambassador in the Soviet Union, George Kennan, to President Truman.

When was the 'Long Telegram' sent?

The 'Long Telegram' was sent on 22nd February, 1946.

Who sent the 'Long Telegram'?

George Kennan, the US Ambassador in the Soviet Union, sent the 'Long Telegram'.

Where was the 'Long Telegram' sent?

The 'Long Telegram' was sent to Washington from the United States Embassy in Moscow.

What did the 'Long Telegram' say?

The 'Long Telegram' stated:

- ✅ The USSR was a threat to capitalism and should be eliminated.
- ✅ The USSR was building its military power.
- ✅ Peace between the USA and the USSR was not possible.
- ✅ The USSR was determined to expand.

THE IRON CURTAIN SPEECH, 1946

'From Stettin in the Baltic to Trieste in the Adriatic, an iron curtain has descended across the continent.'
Winston Churchill, 1946

What was the 'Iron Curtain' speech?

Winston Churchill, although no longer the prime minister of Britain, gave a significant speech where he described how Europe had been divided by an 'iron curtain'. This analogy described the USSR's actions in eastern Europe that had divided Europe in two.

When was the 'Iron Curtain' speech delivered?

Winston Churchill gave the speech in March 1946.

Who delivered the 'Iron Curtain' speech?

Winston Churchill gave the 'Iron Curtain' speech.

Where was the 'Iron Curtain' speech delivered?

Winston Churchill gave the speech in Fulton, USA.

What important argument was made by Churchill during the 'Iron Curtain' speech?

Churchill argued that:

- ☑ Strong American-British relations were essential to stop the spread of communism and maintain peace.
- ☑ The USA must play an active role in world affairs.

Why was the 'Iron Curtain' speech important?

It helped bolster American and western European opposition to communism and the Soviet Union. It worsened relations between the USSR and the West.

How did Stalin respond to the 'Iron Curtain' speech?

Stalin responded to the 'Iron Curtain' speech by:

- ☑ Comparing Churchill to Hitler and claiming Churchill was attempting to draw racial boundaries.
- ☑ Calling Churchill a warmonger (someone who encourages or seeks war).

DID YOU KNOW?

The 'Iron Curtain' speech is officially named 'The Sinews of Peace'.

Churchill gave the speech at Westminster College in Fulton, Missouri.

THE TRUMAN DOCTRINE, 1947

'I believe that we must assist free peoples to work out their own destinies in their own way.'
President Harry Truman, 1947

What was the Truman Doctrine?

The Truman Doctrine was an American policy which was anti-communist and involved the containment of communism. It led to the Marshall Plan *(p.23)*.

When did the Truman Doctrine begin?

President Harry S Truman announced his doctrine on 12th March, 1947.

Why was the Truman Doctrine established?

There were 3 main reasons the Truman Doctrine was created:

- ☑ Britain could not afford to give any more military support to the Greek government in the civil war against Greek communists.
- ☑ The USA promised $400 million in aid to Greece and Turkey to help win the war against the Greek communists.
- ☑ It aimed to contain the spread of communism by giving military and economic assistance to any country threatened by communism.

What were the main points of the Truman Doctrine?

The Truman Doctrine contained 3 key points:

- ☑ It stated the world had a choice between communism, or capitalism and democracy;
- ☑ The USA would send troops and economic aid to countries threatened by communism so it was contained and could not spread;
- ☑ The USA would no longer follow an isolationist foreign policy and would now get involved in the affairs of other countries, rather than stay out of them.

What conditions were there in order for countries to receive aid under the Truman Doctrine?

Countries had to choose capitalism over communism in order to receive aid from the USA.

What was the importance of the Truman Doctrine?

There were 4 main reasons the Truman Doctrine was important:

- ☑ It meant the USA officially abandoned its isolationist foreign policy and would play an active role in the world.
- ☑ It meant the USA was on a potential collision course with the USSR as the doctrine was directed against the spread of communism.
- ☑ It directly resulted in the creation of the Marshall Plan *(p.23)*.
- ☑ It resulted in the further deterioration in the relationship between the USA and the USSR.

DID YOU KNOW?

Harry S Truman's middle name was, literally, 'S'.
It was included to honour his grandfathers, who both had 'S' in their names.

Quizzes, amazing exam preparation tools and more at GCSEHistory.com

THE MARSHALL PLAN, 1947

'The United States should do whatever it is able to do to assist in the return of normal economic health in the world, without which there can be no political stability...'
General George Marshall, 1947

What was the Marshall Plan?
The Marshall Plan was a scheme to provide economic aid to Europe.

When was the Marshall Plan introduced?
The Marshall Plan was introduced in 1948.

Who came up with the Marshall Plan?
It was proposed by the US Secretary of State, George C Marshall.

Why was the Marshall Plan introduced?
The Marshall Plan was essentially the Truman Doctrine *(p.22)* in action. By making countries dependent on US dollars, it would prevent the spread of communism.

How much money was provided by the Marshall Plan?
$13.3 billion was provided by the USA to help rebuild Europe.

Which countries received aid under the Marshall Plan?
A total of 16 western European countries, including France, West Germany and Britain, received aid.

What was it hoped would be achieved by the Marshall Plan?
It was feared the damage and poverty caused by the Second World War would encourage people to turn to communism. Giving countries money to rebuild would stop them becoming communist.

What were the conditions needed to receive aid from the Marshall Plan?
In order to receive money, countries had to trade with the USA and be capitalist.

What was the reaction to the Marshall Plan?
The USSR reacted in 4 main ways to the Marshall Plan:
- ☑ The Soviet Union saw both the Truman Doctrine *(p.22)* and the Marshall Plan as a threat to communism.
- ☑ Stalin called it 'dollar imperialism' and claimed the USA was trying to take over Europe using its economic strength.
- ☑ Stalin responded by creating Cominform *(p.28)* in 1947, which coordinated and controlled communist parties in Europe from the USSR.
- ☑ Comecon *(p.29)* was established in 1949 to organise economic trade between eastern Europe and the USSR.

What was the significance of the Marshall Plan?
The Marshall Plan was significant for 4 key reasons:
- ☑ It helped the economic recovery of western Europe.
- ☑ It limited the expansion of Soviet influence in Europe so the USSR was 'contained'.
- ☑ It deepened the divide between western Europe and eastern Europe as they were now divided politically and economically.

☑ It worsened the relationship between the USA and the USSR.

THE USSR AND THE CREATION OF SATELLITE STATES

'Everyone imposes his own system as far as his army has power to do so. It cannot be otherwise.'
Joseph Stalin, 1945

What were the Soviet satellite states?

The Soviet satellite states were countries in eastern Europe under the political, economic and military influence of the USSR.

Who were the Soviet satellite states?

They were Poland, Czechoslovakia, Hungary, Romania, Bulgaria and East Germany.

When were the Soviet satellite states created?

The satellite states were created between 1946 and 1949.

What methods were used to create the Soviet satellite states?

There are 2 key things to note about the methods used:

☑ In the late 1940s, Stalin installed communist leaders in eastern European countries using 'salami tactics'.

☑ The term 'salami tactics' was coined by the communist Hungarian leader, Matyas Rakosi, to describe how Stalin dea with opposition 'slice by slice'.

How were the Soviet satellite states created?

There were 5 main ways in which the Soviet Union took over eastern European countries:

☑ The Red Army supported communists and intimidated the opposition. They acted as an occupying force.

☑ Elections were held and as a result the communists were part of coalition governments.

☑ The communists worked in coalitions to undermine the government and held key positions, such as head of the police, so they could arrest and murder opponents.

☑ Propaganda was used to label any opposition party or leader a fascist to boost support for communist parties or to demonise democratic politicians.

☑ Once in government, communist parties, aided by the security forces, rigged elections to ensure they remained in power.

What was the importance of the Soviet satellite states?

The satellite states helped the Soviet Union in 4 key ways:

☑ It meant the USSR had gained a large territory with which it could trade.

☑ They enhanced its power.

☑ In theory, they strengthened communism.

☑ They acted as a buffer zone to protect the USSR from invasion.

Quizzes, amazing exam preparation tools and more at GCSEHistory.com

What were the different points of view about the Soviet satellite states?

There are 2 key things to note about how satellite states are viewed:

- ✅ Stalin viewed the satellite states as a necessary buffer against future invasion from Germany in particular.
- ✅ However, Britain and the USA saw them as a threat to the West.

> **DID YOU KNOW?**
> ———————————————
> Despite sharing a border with the USSR, Finland was neither communist nor a satellite state.

THE CREATION OF POLAND AS A SATELLITE STATE, 1947

'Fitting communism onto Poland is like putting a saddle on a cow.'
Stalin, 1944

What is Poland?

Poland is a country in central Europe.

 When did Poland become a satellite state?

Soviet control was established over Poland in 1947.

 How did Poland become a satellite state?

Poland became a satellite state through 5 key events:

- ✅ Before the Second World War, Poland had a mostly agricultural economy and a traditional hatred of the USSR.
- ✅ During the Second World War, it was at first divided between Germany and the USSR, and then completely occupied by Germany.
- ✅ During the war, it had two governments - one based in London, and the other in the Polish town of Lublin.
- ✅ After it was liberated, Soviet troops remained and a new government was formed in June 1945 dominated by communist-sympathising 'Lublin' Poles.
- ✅ Opposition leaders were assassinated and imprisoned before a rigged vote in 1947 gave the communists 80% of the vote.

> **DID YOU KNOW?**
> ———————————————
> **In August 1941, the USSR released thousands of Poles who had been taken prisoner in 1939.**
> They formed eight divisions of the 'Anders Army' and fought alongside British troops in the Middle East.

THE CREATION OF ROMANIA AS A SATELLITE STATE, 1947

*'So far as Britain is concerned, how would it do for you to have 90% predominance in Romania, for
us to have 90% of the say in Greece?'*
Churchill to Stalin in 1944, in the so-called 'Percentages Agreement'

 What is Romania?

Romania is a south-eastern European country.

 When did Romania become a satellite state?

Soviet control was established in Romania in 1947.

How did Romania become a satellite state?

Romania became a satellite state through 4 key events:

- ☑ Romania was a monarchy with little support for communism. During the Second World War it was a German ally.
- ☑ Soviet troops remained there after the war. The Soviets accepted a coalition government in 1945 with communists in key positions.
- ☑ The communists gradually took over the police, and rigged elections in 1946 gave them 90% of the vote.
- ☑ The main opposition leader was subject to a 'show trial' in October 1947 and King Michael was forced to abdicate.

DID YOU KNOW?

In 1945 and 1946, King Michael of Romania went on a 'royal strike' and refused to sign laws made by the communist government.

He was forced to abdicate shortly after attending the wedding of Queen Elizabeth II and Prince Philip in 1947.

THE CREATION OF BULGARIA AS A SATELLITE STATE, 1947

'I feel deep anxiety because of...[the USSR's] overwhelming influence in the Balkans.'
Churchill to Truman, 1945

 What is Bulgaria?

Bulgaria is a country in south-eastern Europe.

 When did Bulgaria become a satellite state?

Bulgaria came under Soviet control in 1947.

 How did Bulgaria become a satellite state?

Bulgaria became a satellite state through 5 key events:

- ☑ Before the Second World War, Bulgaria was a monarchy with strong links to Russia. However, during the war it was allied with Germany.
- ☑ Soviet troops remained there after the war.

Quizzes, amazing exam preparation tools and more at GCSEHistory.com

- The communists joined the Fatherland Front, a coalition government with other parties. However, they then purged it of other political groups.
- The monarchy was abolished in 1946.
- In 1947 a new constitution destroyed democracy and outlawed opposition parties.

> ### DID YOU KNOW?
>
> The Fatherland Front in Bulgaria was originally an anti-Nazi resistance group during the Second World War.

THE CREATION OF CZECHOSLOVAKIA AS A SATELLITE STATE, 1948

'Victorious February!'
Name given to the month in which Czechoslovakia became communist

What was Czechoslovakia?

Czechoslovakia was a country in central Europe.

When did Czechoslovakia become a satellite state?

Czechoslovakia came under Soviet control in 1948.

How did Czechoslovakia become a satellite state?

Czechoslovakia became a satellite state through 5 key events:

- Czechoslovakia had a democracy and strong support for the communists before the war. It was invaded by Germany in 1939.
- After the war, Soviet troops left the country and elections put the communists in charge of a coalition government.
- The communists gradually took control of government ministries.
- Communists arrested political opponents and Jan Masaryk, a non-communist politician, was murdered in March 1948.
- All non-communist members of the government resigned in February 1948, and the communists assumed complete control.

> ### DID YOU KNOW?
>
> **In March 1948, during a communist purge of the Czechoslovakian government, the pro-American Jans Masaryk was found dead beneath his window.**
>
> The Soviets claimed he jumped.

THE CREATION OF HUNGARY AS A SATELLITE STATE, 1948

'Hungary conquered and in chains.'
Albert Camus

What is Hungary?

Hungary is a landlocked country in central Europe.

When did Hungary become a satellite state?

Soviet control was established over Hungary in 1948.

How did Hungary become a satellite state?

Hungary became a satellite state through 6 key events:

- ☑ Hungary had an agricultural-based economy and little support for the communists. It was a German ally in the Second World War.
- ☑ Soviet troops remained in the country after liberation.
- ☑ In November 1945, elections gave communists 17% of the vote, but they were put in control of the Ministry of the Interior.
- ☑ They used secret police to control and intimidate opposition politicians.
- ☑ In 1947 rigged elections gave the communists control of the coalition government.
- ☑ The Social Democratic Party and Communist Party merged in 1948, giving the communists control of Hungary.

DID YOU KNOW?

The communist leader of Hungary was Matyas Rakosi.

He was known by Hungarians as 'the Bald Butcher'.

COMINFORM, 1947

The Communist Information Bureau

What was Cominform?

Cominform was the Communist Information Bureau. It organised all communist parties in Europe under the USSR's control.

When was Cominform created?

The Communist Information Bureau was created in September 1947.

Who were the members of Cominform?

Members included the USSR, France, Italy, Czechoslovakia, Bulgaria, Poland, Yugoslavia and Romania.

Why was Cominform created?

Cominform was created for 2 key reasons:

- ✅ It was a reaction to the creation of the Marshall Plan *(p.23)* by the USA.
- ✅ It was a way in which the USSR could control all communist parties in Europe.

Why was Cominform important?

Cominform meant that the USSR politically controlled all communist parties in eastern Europe. It created a trade network between communist countries.

> **DID YOU KNOW?**
> ――――――――――――――――――――
> **The leader of Yugoslavia, General Tito, resisted being controlled by Cominform.**
> As a result, he was expelled from the Bureau in 1948.

COMECON, 1949

The Soviet Council for Mutual Economic Assistance

What was Comecon?

Comecon was the Council for Mutual Economic Assistance. It was the Soviet Union's alternative to the Marshall Plan *(p.23)*.

When was Comecon created?

Comecon was created in January 1949.

Who was part of Comecon?

Comecon included the Soviet Union, Bulgaria, Czechoslovakia, Poland, Romania, Hungary, Albania and the German Democratic Republic (East Germany).

Why was Comecon created?

Comecon was a reaction to the Marshall Plan *(p.23)*, introduced by the USA, and was created for 2 main reasons:

- ✅ Stalin wanted to reduce any possible economic influence the USA could have on eastern Europe's communist countries by creating his own version of the Marshall Plan *(p.23)*.
- ✅ It was a method of controlling the satellite states in eastern Europe by tying them into close trading relationships with the USSR and each other.

What was the importance of Comecon?

Comecon, with the Marshall Plan *(p.23)*, divided Europe into two economic spheres of influence; western European was capitalist and eastern European was communist.

> **DID YOU KNOW?**
> ――――――――――――――――――――
> In 1972, Cuba became the ninth full member of Comecon.

NATO, 1949

'A shield against aggression.'
President Harry Truman, 1949

What is NATO?

NATO is an acronym for North Atlantic Treaty Organisation. It is a military alliance based on the promise of mutual defence against an attack by an external force.

When was NATO formed?

NATO was formed on 4th April, 1949.

Who joined NATO?

The original 12 members were: the USA, Canada, Great Britain, Belgium, France, Italy, the Netherlands, Norway, Denmark, Luxembourg, Portugal and Iceland.

Why was NATO created?

NATO was formed by the USA and other western countries for 2 main reasons:

- ✅ Stalin and USSR's actions in the Berlin Blockade *(p.33)* had worried them.
- ✅ They wanted military protection from future aggression.

What were the consequences of the creation of NATO?

There were 4 key consequences of the creation of NATO:

- ✅ The USSR was contained in Europe, ensuring if it attacked any European member of NATO the other members would help the country under attack.
- ✅ All NATO members were protected by the promise of mutual military aid against any Soviet attack, helping to make the security of western Europe stronger.
- ✅ In response to West Germany joining NATO, the Soviet Union formed the Warsaw Pact *(p.31)* in 1955 so the USSR had full military control over eastern Europe.
- ✅ The USA had committed to a military presence in Europe.

What message was sent by the creation of NATO?

The creation of NATO sent 2 main messages to the USSR:

- ✅ The USA and western European countries would not accept Soviet aggression.
- ✅ The West would maintain the idea of containment set out in the Truman Doctrine *(p.22)*.

Why was NATO important?

NATO was important for 2 main reasons:

- ✅ It was based on the idea of 'collective security' - when one country is attacked, the rest must assist it.
- ✅ It acted as a deterrent to a military attack by the Soviet Union on western Europe.

DID YOU KNOW?

General Dwight Eisenhower - later US President Eisenhower - became the first Supreme Allied Commander of NATO in 1951.

Quizzes, amazing exam preparation tools and more at GCSEHistory.com

THE WARSAW PACT, 1955

The communist military alliance

What was the Warsaw Pact?

The Warsaw Pact was a defensive military alliance between the USSR and eastern European countries.

When was the Warsaw Pact signed?

The Warsaw Pact was established on 14th May, 1955.

Who was part of the Warsaw Pact?

The members of the Warsaw Pact were the USSR, Albania, Bulgaria, Czechoslovakia, East Germany, Hungary, Poland and Romania.

Why was the Warsaw Pact created?

There were 2 key reasons the Warsaw Pact was created:

- ✅ The USSR felt threatened when West Germany was allowed to join NATO *(p.30)* in 1955 because Germany had invaded Russia in both world wars.
- ✅ The Pact would increase the USSR's control over eastern Europe.

What did the members of the Warsaw Pact agree to?

By joining the Warsaw Pact, members agreed to defend each other if they were attacked by a non-member. This was the idea of collective security.

What were the consequences of the creation of the Warsaw Pact?

There were 3 main consequences of the creation of the Warsaw Pact:

- ✅ The USSR increased control over the satellite states in eastern Europe because it dominated the Pact.
- ✅ Europe was now divided politically, economically and militarily into two hostile camps.
- ✅ It intensified the arms race with the West.

DID YOU KNOW?

Despite having a communist government, Yugoslavia was never a member of the Warsaw Pact.

Albania joined, but was expelled in 1962.

THE MILITARY ARMS RACE AFTER 1945

'I think the bomb instead constitutes merely a first step in a new control by man over the forces of nature too revolutionary and dangerous to fit into old concepts.'
Henry Stimson

What was the arms race?

The arms race was a competition between the USA and the USSR to gain military dominance by developing their nuclear capabilities and weapons.

When was the arms race?

The Soviet Union emerged as a nuclear power in 1949, leading to the arms race with the USA. This lasted until the end of the Cold War *(p.14)* in 1990.

What was the importance of the arms race?

The arms race was important for 2 main reasons:

- ☑ It led to the fear of mutually assured destruction as both sides had enough weapons to destroy the world many times over.
- ☑ The USA and the USSR had to find ways to solve disputes that did not result in a nuclear war.

What were the most important events of the arms race?

There were 6 main military achievements and events during the arms race:

- ☑ 1945 - the USA dropped atomic bombs on Hiroshima and Nagasaki, bringing the Second World War to an end.
- ☑ 1949 - the USSR tested an atomic bomb.
- ☑ 1952 - the USA developed the hydrogen bomb.
- ☑ 1953 - the USSR tested its own hydrogen bomb.
- ☑ 1957 - both the USA and USSR successfully tested intercontinental ballistic missiles (ICBMs).
- ☑ 1962 - the Cuban Missile Crisis was the highest point of tension in the arms race.

What role did brinkmanship play in the arms race?

Brinkmanship was important in the arms race because:

- ☑ An enemy could be forced to back down in a moment of crisis by pushing it to the brink of an unwanted war.
- ☑ To make any threats credible, both sides needed nuclear weapons.
- ☑ The Cuban Missile Crisis is an example of brinkmanship. The USA and the USSR were very close to a nuclear war, with both sides threatening conflict until the USSR backed down.

What was the theory of mutually assured destruction, or MAD in the arms race?

Mutually assured destruction, or MAD, was the following theory:

- ☑ It had developed by the 1960s.
- ☑ It stated that if either the USA or the USSR used their nuclear weapons, both would be destroyed. Each possessed so many, the damage would be unimaginable.
- ☑ It was believed war would be prevented because both sides feared it; a nuclear war was, in theory, unwinnable.

What was nuclear utilisation target selection in the arms race?

Nuclear utilisation target selection theory, or NUTs:

- ☑ Developed in the 1980s.

☑ Was a theory President Reagan believed in. He thought a limited nuclear war was possible as long as the USA struck at the USSR first and wiped out its nuclear weapons.

What were intercontinental ballistic missiles in the arms race?

Intercontinental ballistic missiles, called ICBMs, were nuclear-armed ballistic missiles with a range of more than 3,500 miles.

What were anti-ballistic missiles in the arms race?

Anti-ballistic missiles were missiles that would intercept and destroy other ballistic missiles. The USA and the USSR developed ABMs in the 1960s.

What were multiple independent reentry vehicles in the arms race?

Multiple independent reentry vehicles (MIRVs) were developed in 1968. These missiles carried multiple warheads which could each be independently targeted.

DID YOU KNOW?

In October 1961, the USSR tested its largest nuclear weapon, the Tsar Bomba, creating the most powerful man-made explosion ever seen.

The explosion yielded 58 megatons of TNT and blast waves were recorded as travelling three times around the earth.

THE BERLIN BLOCKADE, 1948-49

'The crisis was planned in Washington, behind a smokescreen of anti-Soviet propaganda.'
Soviet commentary on the Berlin Crisis

What was the Berlin Blockade?

The USSR closed all road, rail and river transport links into West Berlin. This stopped all supplies getting into the city. British, French and US troops were asked to leave.

When was the Berlin Blockade?

The Berlin Blockade started in June 1948 and ended in May 1949.

What caused the Berlin Blockade?

There were 8 key causes of the Berlin Blockade:

☑ The growing tension between the USA and the USSR over the future of Germany.

☑ The growing tension between the USA and the USSR because of their ideological differences and the start of the Cold War *(p.14)*.

☑ In January 1947, the British and USA joined their zones, creating 'Bizonia'. This broke the agreements made at the Potsdam Conference *(p.19)*.

☑ In December 1947, at the London Conference, Britain, France and the USA met to discuss Germany and decide Germany's new constitution. The USSR was not included.

☑ In March 1948, France's zone joined Bizonia to create 'Trizonia'.

- ☑ The USSR left the Allied Control Commission, accusing the West of breaking the Potsdam agreements. They were angry the London Conference had taken place.
- ☑ In April 1948, Trizonia started to receive Marshall Aid *(p.23)* and began to rebuild.
- ☑ Britain, France and the USA introduced a new 'safe' currency, the Deutschmark, into Trizonia on 23rd June, 1948, which angered the USSR.

What were the consequences of the Berlin Blockade?

There were 3 main consequences of the Berlin Blockade:

- ☑ It prevented supplies reaching West Berlin.
- ☑ It led to the Berlin Airlift *(p.34)* from June 1948 to May 1949, in which the Western powers used airplanes to fly supplies into West Berlin.
- ☑ The relationship between the USSR and the West deteriorated further, eventually leading to the creation of NATO *(p.30)*.

What was the significance of the Berlin Blockade?

The Berlin Blockade was significant for 2 key reasons:

- ☑ The West saw it as an act of aggression by Stalin.
- ☑ It created the first major crisis between the USA and the USSR in the Cold War *(p.14)*.

DID YOU KNOW?

During the Berlin Blockade, 2.5 million citizens in Berlin lost access to food, electricity, medicine or fuel.

THE BERLIN AIRLIFT, 1948-49

'The Berlin Blockade was a move to test our ability and our will to win.'
President Harry Truman, 1949

What did the western powers do in response to the Berlin Blockade?

Western powers responded to the blockade of West Berlin by organising an airlift. Supplies were flown into West Berlin every day.

When was the Berlin Airlift?

The Berlin Airlift saw supplies flown into Berlin every day from 26th June, 1948, to 12th May, 1949.

Why did the Berlin Airlift happen?

There were 3 main reasons the Berlin Airlift occurred:

- ☑ The West did not want to be forced out of West Berlin because Stalin would be able to take over.
- ☑ The USA wanted to contain communism, as promised in the Truman Doctrine *(p.22)*.
- ☑ It was a way to get around the blockade without starting a war.

What happened during the Berlin Airlift?

There were 3 key events during the Berlin Airlift:

- Britain, France and the USA flew in supplies of food, medicine and fuel throughout the Blockade.
- By the end of the Blockade, approximately 8,000 tonnes of supplies were being flown in every day.
- A new airport called Berlin-Tegel was built and a new runway was built at Berlin-Tempelhof to cope with the number of planes flying in supplies.

What were the consequences of the Berlin Airlift?

There were 4 key consequences of the Berlin Airlift:

- Two Germanies were created; The Federal Republic of Germany (West Germany) in May 1949 and the German Democratic Republic (East Germany) in October 1949.
- It led to the USA creating a military alliance called NATO *(p.30)* in April 1949.
- Europe was divided even more: politically (capitalism versus communism), economically (Marshall Aid *(p.23)* versus Comecon *(p.29)*), and now militarily.
- The balance of power became more unstable when the USSR conducted its first successful atomic bomb test in August 1949.

DID YOU KNOW?

During the Berlin airlift, an Allied plane landed in Berlin every minute.

It took twenty to thirty minutes for German staff to unload the aircraft.

GERMANY DIVIDED

'We do not fear that the operations of time may never bring a united Europe, with a reunited Germany at its centre.'
Thomas Mann, 1953

What was the division of Germany?

Germany was split into two countries, the Federal Republic of Germany and the German Democratic Republic.

When was the division of Germany?

Germany was first split into two countries when, in May 1949, the Federal Republic of Germany - popularly known as West Germany - was created. The German Democratic Republic - or East Germany - was formed in October 1949.

Why did the division of Germany happen?

Germany was divided into two countries for 2 key reasons:

- The decisions made at the Yalta and Potsdam Conferences resulted in Germany being split into 4 zones under the control of the USSR, France, Britain and the USA.
- The increasing tension between the Western powers (Britain, France and the USA) and the East (the USSR) over the future of Germany.

How did the division of Germany happen?

There were 6 key events that led to the division of Germany:

- This increased tension resulted in the Berlin Crisis when Stalin blockaded Berlin to force the Western powers out of West Berlin.

- The West responded with the Berlin Airlift *(p.34)*.
- Three days after Stalin called off the blockade, the West decided to formally unite their 3 zones into the Federal Republic of Germany on 8th May, 1949.
- The new parliament, the Bundestag, of the Federal Republic of Germany was founded in Bonn on 14th August, 1949.
- After elections, Konrad Adenauer was appointed the first chancellor of the Federal Republic of Germany on 15th September, 1949.
- The USSR responded by formally turning the eastern zone into the German Democratic Republic in October 1949.

 ## Where were the capital cities after the division of Germany?

There were now 2 capital cities, one in each of the divided Germanies:

- The capital of the Federal Republic of Germany was moved to the city of Bonn.
- The capital of the German Democratic Republic was the eastern sector of Berlin controlled by the USSR after the Second World War.

 ## What was the relationship like between the two Germanies after the division of Germany?

The relationship between the two Germanies was tense for 3 key reasons:

- Each German state recognised only itself as the legitimate German nation.
- The Federal Republic of Germany (West Germany) refused to acknowledge Germany had been divided into two separate countries.
- The German Federal Republic was only recognised as a nation by Eastern Bloc countries and the USSR, not by the Western powers.

DID YOU KNOW?

In 1953 there was an uprising against communist rule in East Germany.

It began with a strike in East Berlin, and grew to involve one million people. Up to 125 people were killed in the fighting.

HOW SERIOUS WAS THE BERLIN BLOCKADE?

'You didn't just fly coal to Berlin and keep a city from freezing and the lights from going out. You inspired at least one German boy to want to be just like you when he grew up.'
US Air Force Colonel Wolfgang Samuel, who was a 13 year-old Berliner during the airlift

 ## How serious were the events of the Berlin Blockade?

Historians debate how serious the events of the Berlin Blockade *(p.33)* were.

 ## Why were the events of the Berlin Blockade serious?

Historians give 4 main arguments why the Berlin Blockade *(p.33)* was serious.

- By cutting the supplies and inflicting great hardship on the people of West Berlin, Stalin was committing an act of war.
- Stalin's aim to force the allies out of West Berlin would have made a considerable difference to the balance of power.
- If West Berlin had turned communist, there were fears that the rest of Germany would follow.
- If the West used force to retaliate, it could have escalated into a full-scale nuclear war.

Why were the events of the Berlin Blockade not serious?

Historians give 3 main arguments why the Berlin Blockade *(p.33)* was not serious.

- ☑ Stalin did not succeed in forcing the allies out of West Berlin, which meant the balance of power remained more equal.
- ☑ Neither side wanted the situation to escalate into a hot war. Stalin's aim was simply to stop the separate development of the German zones.
- ☑ Stalin didn't shoot at the planes flying in to drop supplies, and the US did not use force to destroy the blockade.

DID YOU KNOW?

During the Second World War, Berlin's 37 sewage networks were destroyed.

This led to the spread of diseases such as typhoid and dysentery.

HOW SUCCESSFUL WAS THE WEST IN CONTAINING COMMUNISM IN EUROPE?

'Carry the battle to them... Put them on the defensive and don't ever apologise for anything.'
Harry S Truman

What was the success of containment of communism in Europe up to 1949?

Historians debate how successful the West was in containing communism in Europe.

How was containment in Europe successful?

Historians give 3 main arguments why the West was successful in containing communism in Europe:

- ☑ They refused to pull out of West Berlin and forced Stalin to stand down over the Berlin Blockade *(p.33)*.
- ☑ The Truman Doctrine *(p.22)* and Marshall Plan *(p.23)* helped to prevent communism spreading beyond eastern Europe.
- ☑ NATO *(p.30)* provided a military deterrent to stop communism spreading beyond eastern Europe.

How was containment in Europe unsuccessful?

Historians give 4 main reasons why the West was not successful in containing communism in Europe:

- ☑ The Soviet Union established communism in many eastern European countries by fixing elections.
- ☑ The Red Army's occupation of eastern Europe after the war put them in a very strong position.
- ☑ Stalin refused to allow countries under his influence to accept Marshall aid *(p.23)*, limiting the influence of the West.
- ☑ By creating the German Federal Republic (GDR) Stalin had established a new communist state.

DID YOU KNOW?

The leader of Yugoslavia, General Tito, was communist but resisted control by the USSR.

The USSR produced more negative propaganda about him during the Cold War than it did about America and the west.

WHO WAS TO BLAME FOR THE COLD WAR?

'...the Cold War is in fact a real war in which the survival of the free world is at stake.'
The US National Security Council, 1950

Who caused the Cold War?

Historians debate whether the USA or USSR bore greater responsibility for the outbreak of the Cold War *(p.14)*.

How did the USA cause the Cold War?

Some historians argue the USA was mainly responsible for the start of the Cold War *(p.14)* for 6 key reasons:

- ☑ The Marshall Plan *(p.23)*, the Truman Doctrine *(p.22)*, the policy of containment and the creation of NATO *(p.30)* were seen as aggressive moves.
- ☑ President Truman was openly anti-communist, which caused greater tension. His relationship with Stalin was much worse than that of Roosevelt, his predecessor.
- ☑ The USA didn't inform the Soviets about their work on developing the atom bomb. The Soviets found out through their spies and felt betrayed.
- ☑ Stalin was not consulted over the formation of Trizonia or the adoption of the Deutschmark, despite agreement that decisions over Germany would be made jointly.
- ☑ Stalin saw the USA's refusal to leave West Berlin as a threat.
- ☑ Both sides participated in the nuclear arms race.

How did the USSR cause the Cold War?

Some historians argue the USSR was mainly responsible for causing the Cold War *(p.14)* for 6 key reasons:

- ☑ Stalin went against some of the promises he made at Yalta, such as occupying Poland and refusing to allow eastern European countries to have free elections.
- ☑ Instead of free elections in eastern Europe, Stalin ensured communist puppet governments - which he could control - gained power. This happened in Czechoslovakia, Poland, Hungary, Romania, Bulgaria and East Germany. This was seen as a threat to capitalism.
- ☑ The Red Army's occupation of eastern Europe was seen as a threat, and an attempt to control the whole of Europe.
- ☑ Comecon *(p.29)*, Cominform *(p.28)* and the Warsaw Pact *(p.31)* were seen as aggressive moves.
- ☑ The Berlin Blockade *(p.33)* was an extremely aggressive act.
- ☑ Both sides participated in the nuclear arms race.

DID YOU KNOW?

Soviet archives about the Cold War in the USSR were opened in 1991.

This had a huge impact on historical interpretations of the conflict.

Quizzes, amazing exam preparation tools and more at GCSEHistory.com

A

Abdicate - to give up a position of power or a responsibility.

Abolish, Abolished - to stop something, or get rid of it.

Aggression - angry, hostile or violent behaviour displayed without provocation.

Agricultural - relating to agriculture.

Alliance - a union between groups or countries that benefits each member.

Allies - parties working together for a common objective, such as countries involved in a war. In both world wars, 'Allies' refers to those countries on the side of Great Britain.

Assassinate - to murder someone, usually an important figure, often for religious or political reasons.

B

Blockade - a way of blocking or sealing an area to prevent goods, supplies or people from entering or leaving. It often refers to blocking transport routes.

Brinkmanship - pushing a disagreement to its limits in the hope the other side backs down, especially pertaining to war.

Buffer - a protective barrier.

Buffer zone - a neutral area of land to separate hostile forces or nations and provide protection. In the Cold War, Eastern Europe was the buffer zone between Western Europe and the USSR.

C

Capitalism - the idea of goods and services being exchanged for money, private ownership of property and businesses, and acceptance of a hierarchical society.

Chancellor - a senior state official who, in some countries, is the head of the government and responsible for the day-to-day running of the nation.

Claim - someone's assertion of their right to something - for example, a claim to the throne.

Coalition government - a government formed by more than one political party.

Coalition, Coalitions - a temporary alliance, such as when a group of countries fights together.

Collective security - a policy adopted by the League of Nations, with the idea members should feel safe from attack as all nations agreed to defend each other.

Colonialism - when a country seeks to bring other territories under its control, often with the aim of dominating its economy. Religion and cultural practices may also be imposed.

Communism - the belief, based on the ideas of Karl Marx, that all people should be equal in society without government, money or private property. Everything is owned by by the people, and each person receives according to need.

Communist - a believer in communism.

D

Constitution - rules, laws or principles that set out how a country is governed.

Containment - meaning to keep something under control or within limits, it often refers to the American idea of stopping the spread of communism.

Currency - an umbrella term for any form of legal tender, but most commonly referring to money.

D

Demilitarised - to remove all military forces from an area and forbid them to be stationed there.

Democracy - a political system where a population votes for its government on a regular basis. The word is Greek for 'the rule of people' or 'people power'.

Democratic - relating to or supporting the principles of democracy.

Deterrent - something that discourages an action or behaviour.

Dispute - a disagreement or argument; often used to describe conflict between different countries.

Doctrine - a stated principle of government policy; can also refer to a set of beliefs held and taught by a church, political party or other group.

Dollar imperialism - a phrase used by the Soviet Union's Foreign Minister, Molotov, in accusing the USA of using its economic strength to take over Europe through the Marshall Plan.

E

Economic - relating to the economy; also used when justifying something in terms of profitability.

Economy - a country, state or region's position in terms of production and consumption of goods and services, and the supply of money.

Embassy - historically, a deputation sent by one ruler, state or country to another. More recently, it is also the accepted name for the official residence or offices of an ambassador.

F

Fascist - one who believes in fascism.

Foreign policy - a government's strategy for dealing with other nations.

Free elections - elections in which voters are free to vote without interference.

Front - in war, the area where fighting is taking place.

I

Ideology - a set of ideas and ideals, particularly around political ideas or economic policy, often shared by a group of people.

Independence, Independent - to be free of control, often meaning by another country, allowing the people of a nation the ability to govern themselves.

Industrial - related to industry, manufacturing and/or production.

Intercontinental ballistic missile - a guided ballistic missile with a minimum range of 5,500km or 3,400 miles.

Iron Curtain - a phrase used by Winston Churchill to describe the non-physical divide created by Stalin between Eastern Europe and the West.

L

Legitimacy, Legitimate - accepted by law or conforming to the rules; can be defended as valid.

M

Merchant ships - unarmed ships used for carrying supplies and goods.

Military force - the use of armed forces.

Minister - a senior member of government, usually responsible for a particular area such as education or finance.

Monarchy - a form of government in which the head of state is a monarch, a king or queen.

O

Occupation - the action, state or period when somewhere is taken over and occupied by a military force.

P

Parliament - a group of politicians who make the laws of their country, usually elected by the population.

Poverty - the state of being extremely poor.

Predecessor - the person who came before; the previous person to fill a role or position.

Prevent, Preventative, Preventive - steps taken to stop something from happening.

Propaganda - biased information aimed at persuading people to think a certain way.

Prosecute - to institute or conduct legal proceedings against a person or organisation.

Proxy war - a conflict between two sides acting on behalf of other parties who are not directly involved, but who have usually supplied equipment, arms and/or money.

Purged, Purging - abrupt and often violent removal of a group of people from a place or organisation; medically, to make someone sick or induce diarrhoea as a treatment to rid them of illness.

R

Reparations - payments made by the defeated countries in a war to the victors to help pay for the cost of and damage from the fighting.

Revolution - the forced overthrow of a government or social system by its own people.

Rig, Rigged - politically, to interfere in or fix an election to determine the winner.

S

Satellite state - a country under the control of another, such as countries under USSR control during the Cold War.

Soviet - an elected workers' council at local, regional or national level in the former Soviet Union. It can also be a reference to the Soviet Union or the USSR.

Sphere of influence - an area or country under the influence of another country.

State, States - an area of land or a territory ruled by one government.

Strike - a refusal by employees to work as a form of protest, usually to bring about change in their working conditions. It puts pressure on their employer, who cannot run the business without workers.

T

Tactic - a strategy or method of achieving a goal.

Territories, Territory - an area of land under the control of a ruler country.

W

Western powers - a group term used to describe developed capitalist nations, such as Britain and the USA.

INDEX

9 781913 887193